Recess
at 20 Below

Revised Edition

Cindy Lou Aillaud

ALASKA
NORTHWEST
BOOKS®

For all the children who opened my eyes to the possibilities in my own backyard.

A great big hug and thank you to my husband, Whit and my two sons, Jason and Brian, for always being there with your love, support, encouragement, and patience. I am also thankful to all my dear friends that offered assistance when needed. I am forever grateful to my parents, Ron and Lola May Petett, for sending me outside to play! A special thanks to all the children who enjoy *Recess at 20 Below*.

Text and photos © 2005 Cindy Lou Aillaud

Editor: Michelle McCann

First printing of revised edition 2019

Library of Congress Cataloging-in-Publication Data

Names: Aillaud, Cindy Lou, 1955- author.
Title: Recess at 20 below / By Cindy Lou Aillaud. Other titles: Recess at twenty below
Description: Revised edition. | [Anchorage] : Alaska Northwest Books, [2019] | Audience: Age 5. | Audience: K to Grade 3.
Identifiers: LCCN 2018046688 (print) | LCCN 2018052095 (ebook) | ISBN 9781513261935 (ebook) | ISBN 9781513261911 (pbk.) | ISBN 9781513261928 (hardcover)
Subjects: LCSH: Recesses--Alaska--Juvenile literature. | Recesses--Alaska--Juvenile literature--Pictorial works.
Classification: LCC LB3033 (ebook) | LCC LB3033 .A34 2019 (print) | DDC 371.2/4209798--dc23
LC record available at https://lccn.loc.gov/2018046688

Alaska Northwest Books®
An imprint of Graphic Arts Books

GRAPHIC ARTS
BOOKS®

GraphicArtsBooks.com

Proudly distributed by Ingram Publisher Services

GRAPHIC ARTS BOOKS
Publishing Director: Jennifer Newens
Marketing Manager: Angela Zbornik
Editor: Olivia Ngai
Design & Production: Rachel Lopez Metzger

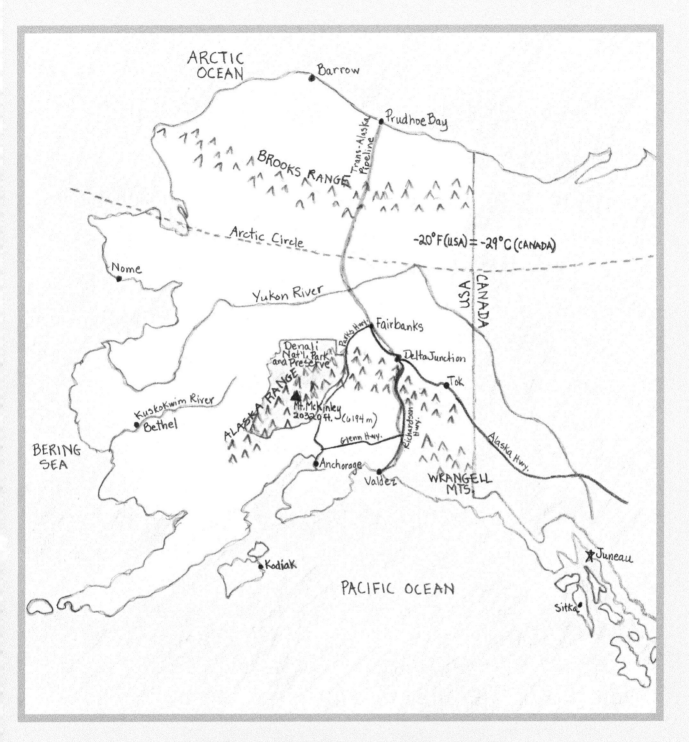

Map by Crystal Finn and Mrs. Aillaud

The cold takes my breath away and makes the inside of my nose stick together, so I tug my scarf up all the way to my eyes. The snow on the ground sparkles like diamonds and the air is filled with tiny ice crystals twinkling out of the sky.

Crunch! Crunch! Crunch! When I walk it sounds like I'm wading through a bag of potato chips. No chance of sneaking up on anyone in this stuff.

I live in Alaska, right along the Alaska Highway. Winter lasts a long, long time here. It seems like forever, but really there's only snow on the ground from September until April. But sometimes we get a snowstorm in May or even in August.

At our school we go out for recess even when it is 20 degrees below zero. We have to wear a LOT of clothes when it gets that freezy.

Getting dressed to go out takes a long time. First, we wiggle and squirm and twist into our thick snow pants.

Then we pull on winter boots and zip our parkas as high as the zippers will go—we don't want any cold air getting in.

Next come the hats. Some hats cover our whole faces so you can only see our eyes and mouths peeking out.

Since we need our fingers to put on all those clothes, our mittens or gloves go on last.

Finally, we're ready to go outside and play. But I can hardly move in all my winter gear—I'm as big as a sumo wrestler! As I waddle down the hall I usually see someone run back to go to the bathroom. Sure hope they make it!

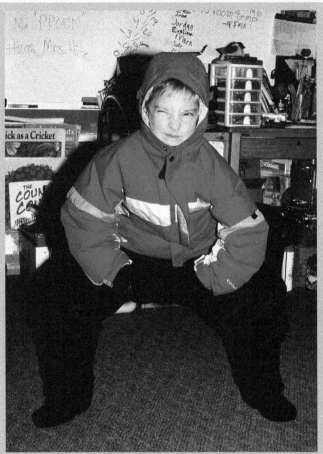

When we get outside I look for my friends. All we can see is each other's eyes, so it helps to remember what colors they are wearing. Samantha reminds me of a giant pickle in her green parka and Megan, who is dressed all in purple, looks like a jar of grape jelly.

It's fun to go sledding during recess. Every time it snows, our maintenance man clears the snow from the school parking lot and dumps it in the middle of the playground. Our sledding hill grows and grows all winter long. After a few months it seems like Denali, the highest mountain in Alaska and North America. We climb to the top and jump on our sleds. *Yippeeeeeeee!*

Sometimes we play on the swings, but by the middle of winter the snow gets so deep there's no room for our legs! We have to throw the swing over the top to make the chains shorter.

And the teeter-totters usually freeze to the ground. *Bang! Bang! Bang!* We have to kick them over and over again to break off the ice.

Before anyone goes down the slide it is covered with ice crystals that sparkle like glitter. It's like sliding down a glacier.

When it's this cold, we have to be careful never to touch our tongue on something metal. It will stick! Then a teacher will have to use a hair dryer or pour a glass of warm water over it to get your tongue free. How embarrassing!

And snowball fights aren't as easy as you might think where the air is so dry. When it's really, really cold our snow is like powder. We can't even make snowballs, but we like to throw it in the air anyway. We toss up puffy snow clouds and swirling tornadoes.

When the wind blows, the snow gets packed hard and then we can break it into chunks, like giant bricks. We stack the chunks to make forts that go high above our heads. Inside our forts, we keep nice and warm, even when the wind is howling outside.

Sometimes we make tunnels in the snow, too. When we pop our heads out, we look just like bear cubs spying on the action. The only bad part is when the snow goes down our backs while we are tunneling. *Brrrrr*, that's cold!

Some days we play soccer or football during recess. Even at 20 below zero you can get too hot. It's hard work running in big heavy boots and thick snow pants. The more we move the warmer we get.

Playing hard means breathing hard. The moisture from our breath floats up to our faces and makes our eyelashes freeze! They feel so thick and heavy, it's hard to even keep them open. The hair around our faces also gets white with frost, so we look old and gray. Some people say that frozen hair will break if you touch it, but mine never has.

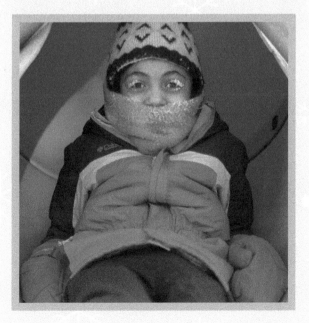

If it's colder than 20 below, we have to stay in for recess. It's too dangerous to be outside then. One day we had to stay inside, but not because it was too cold. We had a visitor on our playground. A moose decided to munch some lunch at our school that day. She came and ate the willow bushes along the fence.

Moose aren't the only wild animals that come to visit. Once I saw a fox sprint through the teeter-totters. Another day ravens attacked our soccer field. Our teacher had drawn some boundary lines with bright red Kool-Aid on the snow. The ravens swooped down out of the sky and gobbled it up!

Our recess is always at noon because it is the sunniest time of the day in my part of Alaska. It isn't very bright though . . . more like early evening. The sun rises and sets in just three hours—it barely peeks above our mountains. We come to school and go home in the pitch-black dark. And if it's cloudy and snowing during recess, the sky gets dark even at noon and it feels like we should get our flashlights out. But it sure makes for good games of hide-and-seek.

By the time the whistle blows to go inside, our cheeks are bright red, our noses are running, and our toes are numb. When we line up we create a cloud of ice fog from everyone breathing in one place. Our breath freezes into tiny specks of ice that hang in the cold air.

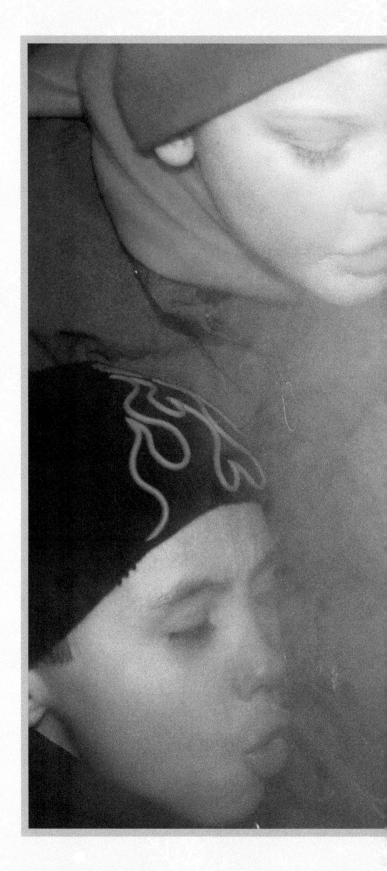

Clomp! Clomp! Clomp!
We sound like a bunch
of elephants walking the
hallways in our big clumsy
boots. When we get to class
we peel off our winter gear.
Lots of us get wild hair
because the air is so dry
and our hair is full of static.
Sometimes we get big shocks,
too, as we pull off our hats.
Ouch! It can really zap!

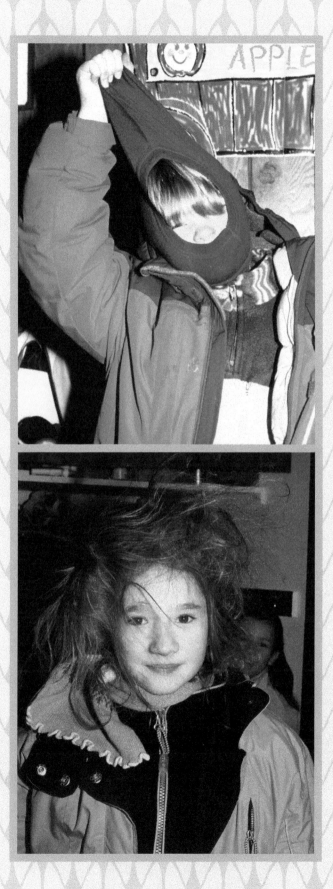

Our classroom sure is a mess with snow pants, parkas, mittens, hats, and boots piled all over the place. Everyone tries to hang up their stuff all at once, so it's easy to get your snow gear mixed up. It seems like we spend hours hunting for the right hat or mitten to hang on our hooks.

When we finally settle into our chairs to begin our afternoon lessons I stare out the frosty window and hope it's not colder than 20 below tomorrow. I can't wait to get back outside and make sure our fort is still there. Or maybe I'll go sledding.

It won't be long until the sun will feel a tiny bit warm during recess. Then we'll see our sledding mountain shrink and we'll hear the drip, drip, drip of melting icicles. We'll stow our sleds until next winter and get ready for the Midnight Sun to chase away the darkness. One day, not too far from now, we'll be riding our bikes past 10 p.m. 'cause the sun will only go down for three hours. But until then, I love recess at 20 below!

Real Questions from Real Kids

Why is it so cold in Alaska?
It's cold in Alaska because Alaska is very far to the north and receives much less heat from the sun than places closer to the equator.

Is Alaska awesome?
I think so! Alaska is the largest state in the United States. It has the largest mountain on the continent. It doesn't have many people living here so there is a lot of wilderness. I hope someday you'll be able to come visit!

Do people live in igloos?
People don't live in igloos, but they are used as temporary shelters by hunters and others who may be stranded in the wilderness.

Do kids ride buses to school in Alaska?
Most of our students in the Delta Junction arrive to school by school bus. Some students have a ½-mile walk just to get to the bus stop. They have to dress warm when it's 40 degrees below zero!

What do the kids do when it gets dark outside and they can't see?
Most kids have a flashlight in their pocket or backpack. Many have headlamps that they use. The snow on the ground also makes it easier to see when it's dark because it reflects moonlight and the auroras when the night is clear.

Have you ever gotten your tongue frozen?

When I was about your age my mom had a can of orange juice thawing on the counter. It had a wonderful layer of ice that formed all around the can (they were metal in those days!). I stuck out my tongue to lick off all that ice and my tongue got stuck! I had to put my tongue with the orange juice can stuck to it underneath the faucet with warm water coming out to get my tongue unstuck!

What would the kids and teachers do if a fox came onto their playground?

Most of the time when a fox visits the playground we are inside the school doing our lessons. When the fox is spotted, everyone gets excited and runs to the windows. It's really fun to watch a fox scampering around the playground! Most foxes are afraid of people so if we are outside at recess they usually run away quickly.

Do other animals visit their schools?

We have had many animals visit our schools. In addition to moose, fox and ravens, we have seen bison, caribou, bears, rabbits, geese, swans, cranes and many other birds.

CPSIA information can be obtained
at www.ICGtesting.com
Printed in the USA
BVHW060002140921
616188BV00011B/6

9 781513 261911